A SEED
A FLOWER
A MINUTE, AN HOUR

A SEED
A FLOWER
A MINUTE, AN HOUR

BY JOAN W. BLOS
ILLUSTRATED BY HANS POPPEL

HALF MOON BOOKS
Published by Simon & Schuster
New York • London • Toronto • Sydney • Tokyo • Singapore

13221

HALF MOON BOOKS
An imprint of Simon & Schuster. 1230 Avenue of the Americas,
New York, New York 10020. Text copyright © 1992 by Joan W. Blos.
Illustrations copyright © 1992 by Hans Poppel. All rights reserved including
the right of reproduction in whole or in part in any form.
Also available in a SIMON & SCHUSTER BOOKS
FOR YOUNG READERS hardcover edition.
Designed by Lucille Chomowicz
The text of this book is set in Futura light.
The illustrations were done in ink and watercolor.
Manufactured in the United States of America

10 9 8 7 6 5 4 3 2 1

Library of Congress Cataloging-in-Publication Data
Blos, Joan W.   A seed, a flower, a minute, an hour/by Joan W. Blos; illustrated
by Hans Poppel. Summary: Illustrations and very brief text depict a seed
changing into a flower, a bee into a swarm, a thought into a poem, and other
changes. [1.Change—Fiction. 2.Stories in rhyme.] I.Poppel, Hans, ill.
II.Title PZ8.B5984Se 1992 [E] —dc20 CIP 91-4992
ISBN 0-671-73214-5   ISBN 0-671-88632-0 (pbk)

For Peter—jwb

To Stephanie—HP

A seed,

a flower.

A minute,

an hour.

A puppy,

a dog.

A tadpole,

a frog.

A cloud,

a storm.

A bee,

a swarm.

A kitten,

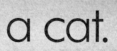

a cat.

A feather,

a hat.

A spark,

a flame.

(A match, the same.)

A thought,

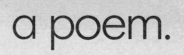

a poem.

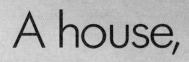

A house,

a home!

A seed, a flower.

A minute, an hour.

A puppy, a dog.

A tadpole, a frog.

A cloud, a storm.

A bee, a swarm.

A kitten, a cat.

A feather, a hat.

A spark, a flame.

(A match, the same.)

A thought, a poem.

A house, a home!